Yummy Meringue Kisses Recipes

Melt In Your Mouth Meringue Kisses That Are Also Delicious

By: Tyler Sweet

License Page

This book or any of its content may not be replicated by any means. Copying, publishing, distributing the contents of this publication without the explicit permission of the author is an infringement of the country's copyright law and will leave you liable to litigation. The contents of this book are well researched and fact-checked before printing to ensure that the readers get the best value. The author is not liable or responsible for the wrongful use of the information provided in the contents of this book.

Table of Contents

Introduction 5

1. Coconut Meringue Kisses 7

2. Raspberry and Pistachios Meringue Kisses 9

3. Lemon Sandwiched Meringue Kisses 11

4. Chocolate and Peppermint Meringue Kisses 13

5. Funfetti Meringue Kisses 15

6. Lime Meringue Kisses 17

7. Chocolate Meringue Kisses 19

8. Mint and Chocolate Sandwiched Meringue Kisses 21

9. Mocha Meringue Kisses 23

10. Pistachio and Cardamom Sandwiched Meringue Kisses 25

11. Rose and Gold Meringue Kisses 28

12. Raspberry Chocolate Meringue Kisses 30

13. Matcha Meringue Kisses 32

14. Red Velvet Meringue Kisses 34

15. Vanilla Bean Meringue Kisses 36

16. Hazelnuts and Coffee Meringue Kisses 38

17. Champagne Meringue 40

18. Pumpkin Spice Meringue Kisses 42

19. Nutella and Chocolate Meringue Kisses 44

20. Almond Meringue Kisses 46

21. Blueberry Swirl Meringue Kisses 48

22. Salted Caramel and Chocolate Meringue Kisses 50

23. Mixed Color Swirl Meringue Kisses 52

24. Lavender and Rose Swirl Meringue Kisses 54

25. Passionfruit Swirl Meringue Kisses 56

26. Pink Marble Swirl Meringue Kisses 58

27. Orange Swirl Meringue Kisses 60

28. Peanut Butter and Chocolate Swirl Meringue Kisses 62

29. Cranberry-Lime Swirl Meringue Kisses 64

30. Strawberry Swirl Meringue Kisses 66

Conclusion 68

Author's Note 70

Introduction

Meringue kisses are cute little yummies that are made out of egg whites. Yes, egg whites if you thought they were only good for fluffy omelets.

Egg whites' ability to contain air when whipped at high speed makes them great for creating airy and jiggly treats like bouncy cakes, fluffy eggs, and many snacks. Meringue kisses is one of those tasty treats that your egg whites could be making.

They are simply a combination of whipped egg whites and sugar, and sometimes a stabilizing agent. When baked, they become such pillowy delights with a crunch and softness that melts in your mouth.

In this cookbook, we explore some fun ways to upgrade the way you enjoy meringue kisses. Whipped egg whites can be transformed into several flavors and here, we do just that.

Come along to unveil a world of meringue kisses that explores delicious aromas and compliments.

1. Coconut Meringue Kisses

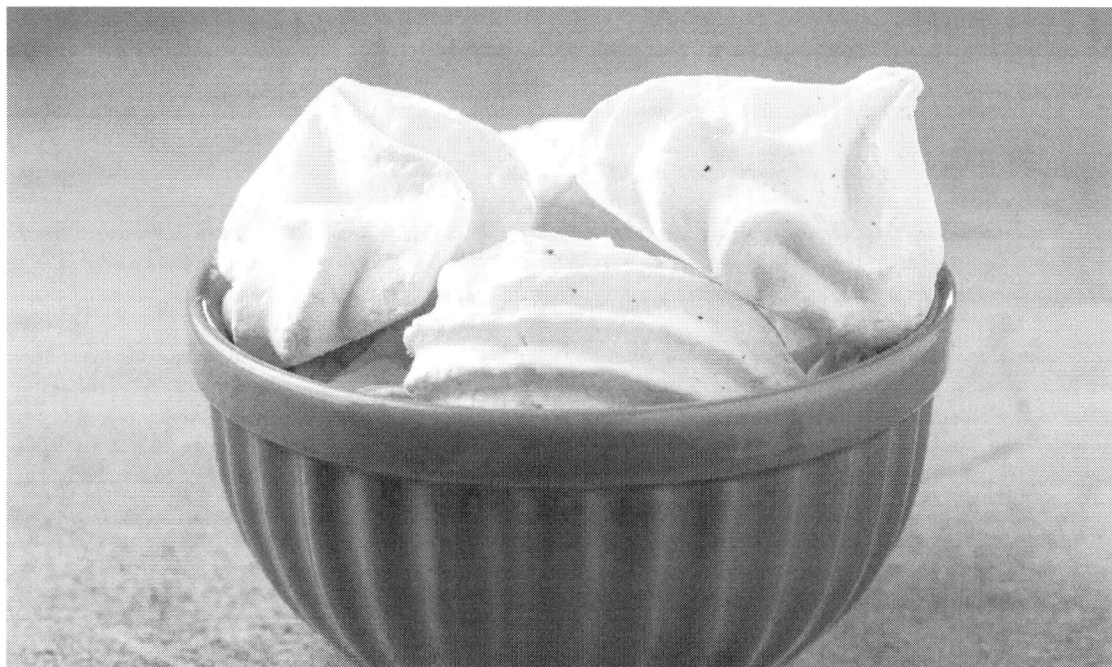

Coconut's aroma is super tropical and summery, which makes these meringue kisses complimentary for sunny days.

Prep Time: 20 mins

Cook Time: 10 mins

Serves: 4+

Ingredients:

- 2 egg whites
- ½ cup caster sugar
- 3 tbsp unsweetened coconut shreds
- Powdered sugar for dusting

Instructions:

Preheat the oven to 300°F. Line two large baking sheets with greaseproof paper and set them aside.

Using an electric mixer, whisk the egg white on high speed until stiff peaks form. While still whisking, gradually add the caster sugar and beat for about 8 minutes or until the sugar dissolves.

Add the shredded coconut and gently fold into the meringue.

Spoon the mixture into a piping bag with a plain or fluted nozzle. On the baking sheets, pipe 1-inch wide swirls with 1-inch intervals between each swirl.

Bake for 8 to 10 minutes or until the meringues are firm. Turn the oven off and let the meringues cool in the oven.

Dust the meringues with powdered sugar and serve.

2. Raspberry and Pistachios Meringue Kisses

Think of raspberry and pistachio cake, and you have a summarized version here. The fusion of fruitiness and nuts is unmatched.

Prep Time: 20 mins

Cook Time: 10 mins

Serves: 4+

Ingredients:

- 4 egg whites
- 1 cup caster sugar
- 1 tablespoon seedless raspberry jam
- ¼ teaspoon red food coloring
- 1 tablespoon finely chopped pistachios

Instructions:

Preheat the oven to 300°F. Line two large baking sheets with greaseproof paper and set them aside.

Using an electric mixer, whisk the egg white on high speed until stiff peaks form. While still whisking, gradually add the caster sugar and beat for about 8 minutes or until the sugar dissolves.

Spoon the mixture into a piping bag with a plain or fluted nozzle. On the baking sheets, pipe 1-inch wide swirls with 1-inch intervals between each swirl.

Add the raspberry jam and red food coloring. Fold until almost smoothly mixed.

Bake for 8 to 10 minutes or until the meringues are firm. Turn the oven off and let the meringues cool in the oven.

Sprinkle the pistachios on the meringue. Serve.

3. Lemon Sandwiched Meringue Kisses

If you've got some lemon curd on hand, you can make one of the most adorable types of meringue kisses, which is this lemon-rich version.

Prep Time: 20 mins

Cook Time: 10 mins

Serves: 4+

Ingredients:

- 1 egg white
- ¼ cup caster sugar
- 2 ½ tbsp lemon curd
- Powdered sugar for dusting

Instructions:

Preheat the oven to 300°F. Line two large baking sheets with greaseproof paper and set them aside.

Using an electric mixer, whisk the egg white on high speed until stiff peaks form. While still whisking, gradually add the caster sugar and beat for about 8 minutes or until the sugar dissolves.

Spoon the mixture into a piping bag with a plain or fluted nozzle. On the baking sheets, pipe 1-inch wide swirls with 1-inch intervals between each swirl.

Bake for 8 to 10 minutes or until the meringues are firm. Turn the oven off and let the meringues cool in the oven.

Sandwich a portion of lemon curd between two meringue kisses and do the same for the remaining meringues. Refrigerate for 30 minutes or more to harden the curd.

Dust with powdered sugar and serve.

4. Chocolate and Peppermint Meringue Kisses

These Christmas minis would be great to have around all through the holidays.

Prep Time: 20 mins

Cook Time: 10 mins

Serves: 4+

Ingredients:

- 2 egg whites
- ½ cup caster sugar
- 1 tsp peppermint extract
- Melted dark or milk chocolate for dipping
- Crushed peppermint candies for decorating

Instructions:

Preheat the oven to 300°F. Line two large baking sheets with greaseproof paper and set them aside.

Using an electric mixer, whisk the egg white on high speed until stiff peaks form. While still whisking, gradually add the caster sugar and beat for about 8 minutes or until the sugar dissolves.

Spoon the mixture into a piping bag with a plain or fluted nozzle. On the baking sheets, pipe 1-inch wide swirls with 1-inch intervals between each swirl.

Bake for 8 to 10 minutes or until the meringues are firm. Turn the oven off and let the meringues cool in the oven.

Dip half of the meringue kisses in the melted chocolate and dip in the crushed peppermint, making sure to coat well. Serve.

5. Funfetti Meringue Kisses

Create a fancy party with your meringue kisses as an altered replica of a classic birthday cake.

Prep Time: 20 mins

Cook Time: 10 mins

Serves: 4+

Ingredients:

- 1 egg white
- ¼ cup caster sugar
- 1 tsp peppermint extract
- Melted dark or milk chocolate for dipping
- Funfetti sprinkles for decorating

Instructions:

Preheat the oven to 300°F. Line two large baking sheets with greaseproof paper and set them aside.

Using an electric mixer, whisk the egg white on high speed until stiff peaks form. While still whisking, gradually add the caster sugar and beat for about 8 minutes or until the sugar dissolves.

Spoon the mixture into a piping bag with a plain or fluted nozzle. On the baking sheets, pipe 1-inch wide swirls with 1-inch intervals between each swirl.

Bake for 8 to 10 minutes or until the meringues are firm. Turn the oven off and let the meringues cool in the oven.

Dip half of the meringue kisses in the melted chocolate and dip in a bowl of funfetti sprinkles.

6. Lime Meringue Kisses

Lime adds a zingy touch to simple meringue kisses, so each bite is a kick.

Prep Time: 20 mins

Cook Time: 10 mins

Serves: 4+

Ingredients:

- 2 egg whites
- ½ cup caster sugar
- 1 tbsp fresh lime juice
- Lime zest for decorating

Instructions:

Preheat the oven to 300°F. Line two large baking sheets with greaseproof paper and set them aside.

Using an electric mixer, whisk the egg white on high speed until stiff peaks form. While still whisking, gradually add the caster sugar and beat for about 8 minutes or until the sugar dissolves. Add the lime juice and slowly whisk in.

Spoon the mixture into a piping bag with a plain or fluted nozzle. On the baking sheets, pipe 1-inch wide swirls with 1-inch intervals between each swirl.

Bake for 8 to 10 minutes or until the meringues are firm. Turn the oven off and let the meringues cool in the oven.

Garnish with the meringue kisses with lime zest and serve.

7. Chocolate Meringue Kisses

Would you call these double-chocolate meringue kisses? Yes, you get a pass with that by dipping chocolate egg whites in silky melted chocolate.

Prep Time: 20 mins

Cook Time: 10 mins

Serves: 4+

Ingredients:

- 2 large egg whites
- ¼ teaspoon cream of tartar
- A pinch of salt
- ½ cup caster sugar
- ¼ cup unsweetened cocoa powder, Dutch-processed
- 2 cups dark chocolate, melted

Instructions:

Preheat the oven to 300°F. Line two large baking sheets with greaseproof paper and set them aside.

Using an electric mixer, whisk the egg whites, cream of tartar, and salt on high speed until stiff peaks form. While still whisking, gradually add the caster sugar and beat for about 8 minutes or until the sugar dissolves.

Sift in the cocoa powder and gently fold in until smooth.

Spoon the mixture into a piping bag with a plain or fluted nozzle. On the baking sheets, pipe 1-inch wide swirls with 1-inch intervals between each swirl.

Bake for 8 to 10 minutes or until the meringues are firm. Turn the oven off and let the meringues cool in the oven.

Dip one meringue kiss on its longer side in the chocolate. Stand the meringue kisses and do the same for the meringue kisses.

Let the chocolate harden in the fridge for a few minutes and serve.

8. Mint and Chocolate Sandwiched Meringue Kisses

Mint and chocolate are perfect festive flavors. So, here's one for your celebratory snack table.

Prep Time: 20 mins

Cook Time: 10 mins

Serves: 4+

Ingredients:

- 2 egg whites
- ½ cup caster sugar
- 1 tsp mint extract
- 1 to 2 drops light green food coloring
- Chocolate sauce for sandwiching

Instructions:

Preheat the oven to 300°F. Line two large baking sheets with greaseproof paper and set them aside.

Using an electric mixer, whisk the egg whites on high speed until stiff peaks form. While still whisking, gradually add the caster sugar and beat for about 8 minutes or until the sugar dissolves. Add the mint extract and green food coloring, and gently whisk in until evenly colored.

Spoon the mixture into a piping bag with a plain or fluted nozzle. On the baking sheets, pipe 1-inch wide swirls with 1-inch intervals between each swirl.

Bake for 8 to 10 minutes or until the meringues are firm. Turn the oven off and let the meringues cool in the oven.

Sandwich a portion of chocolate sauce between two meringues and do the same for the remaining meringues. Serve.

9. Mocha Meringue Kisses

Who loves a good mocha snack or dessert? Mocha's flavor makes such a fine addition to egg whites.

Prep Time: 20 mins

Cook Time: 10 mins

Serves: 4+

Ingredients:

- 2 tablespoons unsweetened cocoa powder
- 1 teaspoon instant espresso powder
- ⅓ cup sifted powdered sugar
- 1 tablespoon cornstarch
- 3 egg whites
- ½ teaspoon vanilla
- ¼ cup caster sugar
- Chocolate sauce for garnish

Instructions:

Preheat the oven to 300°F. Line two large baking sheets with greaseproof paper and set them aside.

Sift the cocoa powder, espresso powder, powdered sugar, and cornstarch on a baking sheet. Set it aside.

Using an electric mixer, whisk the egg whites and vanilla on high speed until stiff peaks form. While still whisking, gradually add the caster sugar and add the sifted espresso mixture, and beat for about 8 minutes or until the sugar dissolves.

Spoon the mixture into a piping bag with a plain or fluted nozzle. On the baking sheets, pipe 1-inch wide swirls with 1-inch intervals between each swirl.

Bake for 8 to 10 minutes or until the meringues are firm. Turn the oven off and let the meringues cool in the oven.

Swirl the chocolate sauce over the meringue kisses and serve.

10. Pistachio and Cardamom Sandwiched Meringue Kisses

These Middle Eastern-inspired meringue kisses don't only have an intense flavor but also feature lemon curd for better tastes.

Prep Time: 20 mins

Cook Time: 10 mins

Serves: 4+

Ingredients:

- 4 egg whites
- 1 cup caster sugar
- 1 tsp cardamom extract
- 1 tsp pistachio extract
- 2 drops light green food coloring
- Lemon curd for sandwiching
- 1 tablespoon finely chopped pistachios

Instructions:

Preheat the oven to 300°F. Line two large baking sheets with greaseproof paper and set them aside.

Using an electric mixer, whisk the egg whites on high speed until stiff peaks form. While still whisking, gradually add the caster sugar and beat for about 8 minutes or until the sugar dissolves.

Spoon the mixture into a piping bag with a plain or fluted nozzle. On the baking sheets, pipe 1-inch wide swirls with 1-inch intervals between each swirl.

Add the cardamom extract, pistachio extract, and green food coloring. Fold until almost smoothly mixed.

Bake for 8 to 10 minutes or until the meringues are firm. Turn the oven off and let the meringues cool in the oven.

Sandwich a portion of lemon curd between two meringues and do the same for the remaining meringues.

Sprinkle the pistachios on the meringue and serve.

11. Rose and Gold Meringue Kisses

How quintessential are these? Such finesse that is awesome for a classy party.

Prep Time: 20 mins

Cook Time: 10 mins

Serves: 4+

Ingredients:

- 2 egg whites
- 1 cup + 2 tbsp caster sugar
- ¼ tsp rose water
- ⅛ tsp salt
- Gold leaf for garnish

Instructions:

Preheat the oven to 300°F. Line two large baking sheets with greaseproof paper and set them aside.

Using an electric mixer, whisk the egg whites on high speed until stiff peaks form. While still whisking, gradually add the caster sugar and beat for about 8 minutes or until the sugar dissolves. Add the rose water and salt, and whisk for another minute.

Spoon the mixture into a piping bag with a plain or fluted nozzle. On the baking sheets, pipe 1-inch wide swirls with 1-inch intervals between each swirl.

Bake for 8 to 10 minutes or until the meringues are firm. Turn the oven off and let the meringues cool in the oven.

Decorate the meringue kisses with bits of the gold leaf. Serve.

12. Raspberry Chocolate Meringue Kisses

Raspberry and chocolate always go well together and don't disappoint here. Their color scheme is also enticing.

Prep Time: 20 mins

Cook Time: 10 mins

Serves: 4+

Ingredients:

- 4 egg whites
- 1 cup caster sugar
- 1 tablespoon seedless raspberry jam
- ¼ teaspoon red food coloring
- ¼ cup freeze-dried raspberries, chopped

Instructions:

Preheat the oven to 300°F. Line two large baking sheets with greaseproof paper and set them aside.

Using an electric mixer, whisk the egg white on high speed until stiff peaks form. While still whisking, gradually add the caster sugar and beat for about 8 minutes or until the sugar dissolves.

Spoon the mixture into a piping bag with a plain or fluted nozzle. On the baking sheets, pipe 1-inch wide swirls with 1-inch intervals between each swirl.

Add the raspberry jam and red food coloring. Fold until almost smoothly mixed.

Bake for 8 to 10 minutes or until the meringues are firm. Turn the oven off and let the meringues cool in the oven.

Dip half of the meringue kisses in the melted chocolate and roll the meringue kisses in the dried-freeze raspberries.

Serve.

13. Matcha Meringue Kisses

Besides factoring some healthy elements, that is matcha powder into meringue kisses, can we talk about how pretty their color is? So heartwarming.

Prep Time: 20 mins

Cook Time: 10 mins

Serves: 4+

Ingredients:

- 2 large egg whites
- ½ cup caster sugar
- A pinch of cream of tartar
- A pinch of salt
- 3 tsp matcha powder mixed with 5 to 6 tsp water

Instructions:

Preheat the oven to 300°F. Line two large baking sheets with greaseproof paper and set them aside.

Using an electric mixer, whisk the egg whites on high speed until stiff peaks form. Add the cream of tartar and salt, and whisk for another minute. While still whisking, gradually add the caster sugar and beat for about 8 minutes or until the sugar dissolves. Add the matcha mixture and whisk until fully incorporated.

Spoon the mixture into a piping bag with a plain or fluted nozzle. On the baking sheets, pipe 1-inch wide swirls with 1-inch intervals between each swirl.

Bake for 8 to 10 minutes or until the meringues are firm. Turn the oven off and let the meringues cool in the oven.

Serve.

14. Red Velvet Meringue Kisses

Who loves a good red velvet cake but isn't up for all that baking process? Simplify the process via meringue kisses and enjoy some good yum.

Prep Time: 20 mins

Cook Time: 10 mins

Serves: 4+

Ingredients:

- 2 teaspoons cocoa powder
- 1 teaspoon red gel food color
- 2 teaspoons water
- 6 large egg whites
- ¼ teaspoon cream of tartar
- ⅛ teaspoon salt
- 1 ½ cups caster sugar
- 1 teaspoon vanilla

Instructions:

Preheat the oven to 300°F. Line two large baking sheets with greaseproof paper and set them aside.

In a bowl, mix the cocoa powder, red food coloring, and water until smooth.

Using an electric mixer, whisk the egg whites on high speed until stiff peaks form. Add the cream of tartar and salt, and whisk for another minute. While still whisking, gradually add the caster sugar and beat for about 8 minutes or until the sugar dissolves. Add the vanilla and whisk until fully incorporated. Fold in the cocoa powder until partially incorporated.

Spoon the mixture into a piping bag with a plain or fluted nozzle. On the baking sheets, pipe 1-inch wide swirls with 1-inch intervals between each swirl.

Bake for 8 to 10 minutes or until the meringues are firm. Turn the oven off and let the meringues cool in the oven.

Serve.

15. Vanilla Bean Meringue Kisses

The classic flavor for meringue kisses is vanilla. Here, rather than using vanilla extract, we use vanilla beans to enrich the vanilla aroma that you get.

Prep Time: 20 mins

Cook Time: 10 mins

Serves: 4+

Ingredients:

- 2 large egg whites
- A pinch of cream of tartar
- A pinch of salt
- ½ cup caster sugar
- 1 vanilla bean, paste extracted

Instructions:

Preheat the oven to 300°F. Line two large baking sheets with greaseproof paper and set them aside.

Using an electric mixer, whisk the egg whites on high speed until stiff peaks form. Add the cream of tartar and salt, and whisk for another minute. While still whisking, gradually add the caster sugar and vanilla paste, and beat for about 8 minutes or until the sugar dissolves.

Spoon the mixture into a piping bag with a plain or fluted nozzle. On the baking sheets, pipe 1-inch wide swirls with 1-inch intervals between each swirl.

Bake for 8 to 10 minutes or until the meringues are firm. Turn the oven off and let the meringues cool in the oven.

Serve.

16. Hazelnuts and Coffee Meringue Kisses

Take a chill with some coffee and these nutty coffee meringue kisses to compliment.

Prep Time: 20 mins

Cook Time: 10 mins

Serves: 4+

Ingredients:

- 4 large egg whites, room temperature
- ¼ tsp white vinegar
- 1 tsp coffee extract
- 1 cup granulated sugar
- 1 cup hazelnut paste, good-quality
- 2 tbsp coffee beans, finely chopped

Instructions:

Preheat the oven to 300°F. Line two large baking sheets with greaseproof paper and set them aside.

Using an electric mixer, whisk the egg whites, vinegar, and coffee extract on high speed until stiff peaks form. While still whisking, gradually add the caster sugar and beat for about 8 minutes or until the sugar dissolves. Remove the whisk and use a spatula to gently fold the hazelnut paste into the meringue.

Spoon the mixture into a piping bag with a plain or fluted nozzle. On the baking sheets, pipe 1-inch wide swirls with 1-inch intervals between each swirl.

Bake for 8 to 10 minutes or until the meringues are firm. Turn the oven off and let the meringues cool in the oven.

Sprinkle the chopped coffee on the meringue kisses and serve.

17. Champagne Meringue

What a fine way to use any excesses of Champagne that you have. These meringue kisses are such special treats for parties and make such an elegant addition to your servings.

Prep Time: 20 mins

Cook Time: 10 mins

Serves: 4+

Ingredients:

- ⅛ teaspoon cream of tartar
- 3 large egg whites
- A dash of salt
- ½ cup superfine sugar
- 2 teaspoons Champagne

Instructions:

Preheat the oven to 300°F. Line two large baking sheets with greaseproof paper and set them aside.

Using an electric mixer, whisk the egg whites on high speed until stiff peaks form. Add the cream of tartar and salt, and whisk for another minute. While still whisking, gradually add the caster sugar and beat for about 8 minutes or until the sugar dissolves.

Add the Champagne and whisk for about 6 minutes or until stiff peak forms.

Spoon the mixture into a piping bag with a plain or fluted nozzle. On the baking sheets, pipe 1-inch wide swirls with 1-inch intervals between each swirl.

Bake for 8 to 10 minutes or until the meringues are firm. Turn the oven off and let the meringues cool in the oven.

Serve.

18. Pumpkin Spice Meringue Kisses

Keep this recipe close by for treating yourself in the fall. The pumpkin spice comes right through and makes them excellent to enjoy with hot spiced chocolate.

Prep Time: 20 mins

Cook Time: 10 mins

Serves: 4+

Ingredients:

- 4 egg whites
- ½ teaspoon cream of tartar
- A pinch of salt
- 1 cup granulated sugar
- ½ teaspoon vanilla extract
- ½ teaspoon maple extract
- 1 teaspoon pumpkin pie spice
- 1 to 2 drops of orange food coloring

Instructions:

Preheat the oven to 300°F. Line two large baking sheets with greaseproof paper and set them aside.

Using an electric mixer, whisk the egg whites on high speed until stiff peaks form. Add the cream of tartar and salt, and whisk for another minute. While still whisking, gradually add the caster sugar and beat for about 8 minutes or until the sugar dissolves.

Add the vanilla extract and maple extracts, pumpkin pie spice, and orange food coloring and whisk for about 6 minutes or until stiff peak forms.

Spoon the mixture into a piping bag with a plain or fluted nozzle. On the baking sheets, pipe 1-inch wide swirls with 1-inch intervals between each swirl.

Bake for 8 to 10 minutes or until the meringues are firm. Turn the oven off and let the meringues cool in the oven.

Serve.

19. Nutella and Chocolate Meringue Kisses

Nutella and chocolate, isn't that too much? No! That's a healthy splurge that we think would work great for meringue kisses. Think of all that goodness.

Prep Time: 20 mins

Cook Time: 10 mins

Serves: 4+

Ingredients:

- 4 large egg whites, room temperature
- ¼ tsp white vinegar
- 1 tsp coffee extract
- 1 cup granulated sugar
- 1 cup Nutella
- Milk chocolate sauce for sandwiching

Instructions:

Preheat the oven to 300°F. Line two large baking sheets with greaseproof paper and set them aside.

Using an electric mixer, whisk the egg whites, vinegar, and coffee extract on high speed until stiff peaks form. While still whisking, gradually add the caster sugar and beat for about 8 minutes or until the sugar dissolves. Remove the whisk and use a spatula to gently fold the hazelnut paste into the meringue.

Spoon the mixture into a piping bag with a plain or fluted nozzle. On the baking sheets, pipe 1-inch wide swirls with 1-inch intervals between each swirl.

Bake for 8 to 10 minutes or until the meringues are firm. Turn the oven off and let the meringues cool in the oven.

Sandwich chocolate sauce between two meringue kisses and do the same for the remaining meringues. Dust with powdered sugar and serve.

20. Almond Meringue Kisses

Right here is an opportunity for you to broaden your love for almonds.

Prep Time: 20 mins

Cook Time: 10 mins

Serves: 4+

Ingredients:

- 4 egg whites
- 1 cup caster sugar
- 2 tsp almond extract
- 1 drop brown food coloring (optional)
- 1 tablespoon finely chopped almonds

Instructions:

Preheat the oven to 300°F. Line two large baking sheets with greaseproof paper and set them aside.

Using an electric mixer, whisk the egg whites on high speed until stiff peaks form. While still whisking, gradually add the caster sugar and beat for about 8 minutes or until the sugar dissolves.

Spoon the mixture into a piping bag with a plain or fluted nozzle. On the baking sheets, pipe 1-inch wide swirls with 1-inch intervals between each swirl.

Add the almond extract and brown food coloring. Fold until almost smoothly mixed.

Bake for 8 to 10 minutes or until the meringues are firm. Turn the oven off and let the meringues cool in the oven.

Sprinkle the almonds on the meringue kisses and serve.

21. Blueberry Swirl Meringue Kisses

Let's get into fancy meringue kisses. Blueberry jam sits pretty on meringue kisses to give you wholesome bites.

Prep Time: 20 mins

Cook Time: 10 mins

Serves: 4+

Ingredients:

- 3 large egg whites
- 1 tsp lemon juice
- ½ tsp cream of tartar
- A pinch of salt
- ¾ cup caster sugar
- 1 cup blueberry sauce

Instructions:

Preheat the oven to 300°F. Line two large baking sheets with greaseproof paper and set them aside.

Using an electric mixer, whisk the egg whites and lemon juice on high speed until stiff peaks form. Add the cream of tartar and salt, and whisk for another minute. While still whisking, gradually add the caster sugar and beat for about 8 minutes or until the sugar dissolves.

Spoon the mixture into a piping bag with a plain or fluted nozzle. On the baking sheets, pipe 1-inch wide swirls with 1-inch intervals between each swirl.

Dot each meringue with a ¼ teaspoon of blueberry sauce and use a toothpick to swirl the sauce into the meringue. The swirl's intensity is up to your preference.

Bake for 8 to 10 minutes or until the meringues are firm. Turn the oven off and let the meringues cool in the oven.

Serve the meringue kisses.

22. Salted Caramel and Chocolate Meringue Kisses

Salted caramel and chocolate just melts the heart. Here, both are swirled atop meringue kisses to give you rich tastes and flavor depth in each bite.

Prep Time: 20 mins

Cook Time: 10 mins

Serves: 4+

Ingredients:

- 3 large egg whites
- ½ tsp cream of tartar
- A pinch of salt
- ¾ cup caster sugar
- ½ cup salted caramel sauce
- ½ cup chocolate sauce

Instructions:

Preheat the oven to 300°F. Line two large baking sheets with greaseproof paper and set them aside.

Using an electric mixer, whisk the egg whites on high speed until stiff peaks form. Add the cream of tartar and salt, and whisk for another minute. While still whisking, gradually add the caster sugar and beat for about 8 minutes or until the sugar dissolves.

Spoon the mixture into a piping bag with a plain or fluted nozzle. On the baking sheets, pipe 1-inch wide swirls with 1-inch intervals between each swirl.

Dot each meringue with a ¼ teaspoon each of salted caramel sauce and chocolate sauce, and use a toothpick to swirl the sauce into the meringue. The swirl's intensity is up to your preference.

Bake for 8 to 10 minutes or until the meringues are firm. Turn the oven off and let the meringues cool in the oven.

Serve the meringue kisses.

23. Mixed Color Swirl Meringue Kisses

Get the kids excited with these playful meringue kisses. They'll actually enjoy making them with you.

Prep Time: 20 mins

Cook Time: 10 mins

Serves: 4+

Ingredients:

- 3 large egg whites
- 1 tsp lemon juice
- ½ tsp cream of tartar
- A pinch of salt
- ¾ cup caster sugar
- Food gel color, colors of your choice

Instructions:

Preheat the oven to 300°F. Line two large baking sheets with greaseproof paper and set them aside.

Using an electric mixer, whisk the egg whites and lemon juice on high speed until stiff peaks form. Add the cream of tartar and salt, and whisk for another minute. While still whisking, gradually add the caster sugar and beat for about 8 minutes or until the sugar dissolves.

Remove the whisk attachment and add 1 to 2 drops each of the food color gels. Using a spatula, gently fold the coloring into the meringue a few times to create a swirl without mixing evenly. The swirl's intensity is up to your preference.

Spoon the mixture into a piping bag with a plain or fluted nozzle. On the baking sheets, pipe 1-inch wide swirls with 1-inch intervals between each swirl.

Bake for 8 to 10 minutes or until the meringues are firm. Turn the oven off and let the meringues cool in the oven.

Serve the meringue kisses.

24. Lavender and Rose Swirl Meringue Kisses

These floral rich meringue kisses are perfect for a lady's snack table. It brings out the femininity in her.

Prep Time: 20 mins

Cook Time: 10 mins

Serves: 4+

Ingredients:

- ⅛ teaspoon cream of tartar
- 3 large egg whites
- A dash of salt
- ½ cup superfine sugar
- ½ tsp lavender extract
- ½ tsp rose extract
- 1 to 2 drops purple food gel color
- 1 to 2 drops red food color gel

Instructions:

Using an electric mixer, whisk the egg whites on high speed until stiff peaks form. Add the cream of tartar and salt, and whisk for another minute. While still whisking, gradually add the caster sugar and beat for about 8 minutes or until the sugar dissolves.

Add the lavender and rose extracts, and whisk for about 6 minutes or until stiff peak forms.

Remove the whisk attachment and add 1 to 2 drops each of the food color gels. Using a spatula, gently fold the coloring into the meringue a few times to create a swirl without mixing evenly. The swirl's intensity is up to your preference.

Spoon the mixture into a piping bag with a plain or fluted nozzle. On the baking sheets, pipe 1-inch wide swirls with 1-inch intervals between each swirl.

Bake for 8 to 10 minutes or until the meringues are firm. Turn the oven off and let the meringues cool in the oven.

Serve the meringue kisses.

25. Passionfruit Swirl Meringue Kisses

Passion fruit's aroma is so amazing and brings a pretty color and summery character to these meringue kisses.

Prep Time: 20 mins

Cook Time: 10 mins

Serves: 4+

Ingredients:

- 3 large egg whites
- A pinch of salt
- 1 tsp lemon juice
- ½ tsp cream of tartar
- ¾ cup caster sugar
- 1 cup passion fruit sauce or curd

Instructions:

Preheat the oven to 300°F. Line two large baking sheets with greaseproof paper and set them aside.

Using an electric mixer, whisk the egg whites and lemon juice on high speed until stiff peaks form. Add the cream of tartar and salt, and whisk for another minute. While still whisking, gradually add the caster sugar and beat for about 8 minutes or until the sugar dissolves.

Spoon the mixture into a piping bag with a plain or fluted nozzle. On the baking sheets, pipe 1-inch wide swirls with 1-inch intervals between each swirl.

Dot each meringue with a ¼ teaspoon of passion fruit sauce or curd and use a toothpick to swirl the sauce into the meringue. The swirl's intensity is up to your preference.

Bake for 8 to 10 minutes or until the meringues are firm. Turn the oven off and let the meringues cool in the oven.

Serve the meringue kisses.

26. Pink Marble Swirl Meringue Kisses

These are pretty! While they are only a merge of meringue and pink food coloring, you can infuse them with rose water for a better depth of flavor. Also, explore different food coloring for varying marbling.

Prep Time: 20 mins

Cook Time: 10 mins

Serves: 4+

Ingredients:

- 3 large egg whites
- 1 tsp lemon juice
- ½ tsp cream of tartar
- A pinch of salt
- ¾ cup caster sugar
- Pink food gel color

Instructions:

Preheat the oven to 300°F. Line two large baking sheets with greaseproof paper and set them aside.

Using an electric mixer, whisk the egg whites and lemon juice on high speed until stiff peaks form. Add the cream of tartar and salt, and whisk for another minute. While still whisking, gradually add the caster sugar and beat for about 8 minutes or until the sugar dissolves.

Spoon the mixture into a piping bag with a plain or fluted nozzle. On the baking sheets, pipe 1-inch wide swirls with 1-inch intervals between each swirl.

Dot each meringue with a little pink food gel color and use a toothpick to swirl the coloring into the meringue. The swirl's intensity is up to your preference.

Bake for 8 to 10 minutes or until the meringues are firm. Turn the oven off and let the meringues cool in the oven.

Serve the meringue kisses garnished with white chocolate crumbles, chopped nuts, etc.

27. Orange Swirl Meringue Kisses

Enjoy a yummy, sunny burst of orange aromas that come through these colorful treats.

Prep Time: 20 mins

Cook Time: 10 mins

Serves: 4+

Ingredients:

- 3 large egg whites
- 2 tsp fresh orange juice
- ½ tsp cream of tartar
- A pinch of salt
- ¾ cup caster sugar
- Orange food gel color

Instructions:

Preheat the oven to 300°F. Line two large baking sheets with greaseproof paper and set them aside.

Using an electric mixer, whisk the egg whites and orange juice on high speed until stiff peaks form. Add the cream of tartar and salt, and whisk for another minute. While still whisking, gradually add the caster sugar and beat for about 8 minutes or until the sugar dissolves.

Remove the whisk attachment and add 1 to 2 drops of the orange food gel color. Using a spatula, gently fold the coloring into the meringue a few times to create a swirl without mixing evenly. The swirl's intensity is up to your preference.

Spoon the mixture into a piping bag with a plain or fluted nozzle. On the baking sheets, pipe 1-inch wide swirls with 1-inch intervals between each swirl.

Bake for 8 to 10 minutes or until the meringues are firm. Turn the oven off and let the meringues cool in the oven.

Serve the meringue kisses.

28. Peanut Butter and Chocolate Swirl Meringue Kisses

Peanut butter and chocolate, definitely a good idea. Throw on some jam and you have something exceptional.

Prep Time: 20 mins

Cook Time: 10 mins

Serves: 4+

Ingredients:

- 3 large egg whites
- ½ tsp cream of tartar
- A pinch of salt
- ¾ cup caster sugar
- ½ cup creamy peanut sauce
- ½ cup chocolate sauce

Instructions:

Preheat the oven to 300°F. Line two large baking sheets with greaseproof paper and set them aside.

Using an electric mixer, whisk the egg whites on high speed until stiff peaks form. Add the cream of tartar and salt, and whisk for another minute. While still whisking, gradually add the caster sugar and beat for about 8 minutes or until the sugar dissolves.

Spoon the mixture into a piping bag with a plain or fluted nozzle. On the baking sheets, pipe 1-inch wide swirls with 1-inch intervals between each swirl.

Dot each meringue with a ¼ teaspoon each of peanut sauce and chocolate sauce, and use a toothpick to swirl the sauce into the meringue. The swirl's intensity is up to your preference.

Bake for 8 to 10 minutes or until the meringues are firm. Turn the oven off and let the meringues cool in the oven.

Serve the meringue kisses.

29. Cranberry-Lime Swirl Meringue Kisses

Another option that's great for the holidays is this cranberry and lime-fused treat. They are nicely tangy with an amazing fruity flavor.

Prep Time: 20 mins

Cook Time: 10 mins

Serves: 4+

Ingredients:

- 3 large egg whites
- 1 tsp lime juice
- ½ tsp cream of tartar
- A pinch of salt
- ¾ cup caster sugar
- 1 cup cranberry sauce

Instructions:

Preheat the oven to 300°F. Line two large baking sheets with greaseproof paper and set them aside.

Using an electric mixer, whisk the egg whites and lime juice on high speed until stiff peaks form. Add the cream of tartar and salt, and whisk for another minute. While still whisking, gradually add the caster sugar and beat for about 8 minutes or until the sugar dissolves.

Spoon the mixture into a piping bag with a plain or fluted nozzle. On the baking sheets, pipe 1-inch wide swirls with 1-inch intervals between each swirl.

Dot each meringue with a ¼ teaspoon of cranberry sauce and use a toothpick to swirl the sauce into the meringue. The swirl's intensity is up to your preference.

Bake for 8 to 10 minutes or until the meringues are firm. Turn the oven off and let the meringues cool in the oven.

Serve the meringue kisses.

30. Strawberry Swirl Meringue Kisses

Strawberry jam atop meringue kisses and you have an irresistible snack.

Prep Time: 20 mins

Cook Time: 10 mins

Serves: 4+

Ingredients:

- 3 large egg whites
- 1 tsp lemon juice
- ½ tsp cream of tartar
- A pinch of salt
- ¾ cup caster sugar
- 1 cup strawberry sauce

Instructions:

Preheat the oven to 300°F. Line two large baking sheets with greaseproof paper and set them aside.

Using an electric mixer, whisk the egg whites and lemon juice on high speed until stiff peaks form. Add the cream of tartar and salt, and whisk for another minute. While still whisking, gradually add the caster sugar and beat for about 8 minutes or until the sugar dissolves.

Spoon the mixture into a piping bag with a plain or fluted nozzle. On the baking sheets, pipe 1-inch wide swirls with 1-inch intervals between each swirl.

Dot each meringue with a ¼ teaspoon of strawberry sauce and use a toothpick to swirl the sauce into the meringue. The swirl's intensity is up to your preference.

Bake for 8 to 10 minutes or until the meringues are firm. Turn the oven off and let the meringues cool in the oven.

Serve the meringue kisses.

Conclusion

Which recipe of meringue kisses would you want to try first?

You know, what's cool? You could mix and match flavors for every batch of meringue kisses that you bake. That way, you have many options to explore and enjoy.

Make batches to store and give to friends, and you just might have found yourself a new hobby.

Biography

"Cooking is a chore unless you love the process", which is the motto of Tyler Sweet, an extremely talented chef who has made her name in the catering industry with the help of her deep understanding of a variety of ingredients and human taste buds. She had always loved whipping up new recipes as a pass time activity but her career began when she got her first job at a local restaurant and realized that she would not mind doing it forever.

Tyler's hobby blossomed into a passion that drove her up the ladder so quickly that by the end of the year, she was already a sous chef and a rising talent. An impeccable eye for unique mixtures and a willingness to learn new dishes, she has since then worked for over 10 five-star restaurants in the tri-state. Presently, Sweet owns a thriving online cooking class where she has found a great, interactive avenue to teach on her most favorite subject, food.

Author's Note

I really appreciate you taking the time to not just download but also read my book, you don't know but that is the highest compliment you can ever give me. And it may seem greedy but I just have one more favor to ask of you, I need your feedback. Do you have any comments, suggestions, or complaints? Or you have an idea for my next book? Please reach out to me if you like, I'm always available for my loyal readers.

Thank you.

Tyler Sweet

Made in United States
Troutdale, OR
02/06/2025

28713369R00040